INCREASE YOUR ANOINTING

INCREASE YOUR ANOINTING
(SECOND EDITION)

Discover the Supernatural

By Bill Vincent

Revival Waves of Glory Books & Publishing has allowed this work to remain exactly as the author intended, verbatim, without editorial input.

All Scripture quotations are from the Authorized King James Version of the Bible unless otherwise noted.

Softcover: 978-0692648889

PUBLISHED BY REVIVAL WAVES OF GLORY BOOKS & PUBLISHING
www.revivalwavesofgloryministries.com
Litchfield, IL

Published in the United States of America

Table of Contents

INTRODUCTION

The Church for centuries has been on a decline from the place it should be. God said that we are to do greater works. Most ministries are not even doing the works of Jesus.

Things are about to change. God has spoken that what I have discovered is being made available so that we can all attain the prize of our high calling. It is time for us to flow in miracles signs and wonders. I'm talking about even in the local Church. Get ready for an increase of the anointing. Remember it is going to cost you something but it will be worth it. You are about to discover three life changing types of anointing. There is the revelatory, the breaker, and the kingly anointing. This is the most important things I discovered that brought a higher level anointing.

THE KINGLY ANOINTING

This is the day we shall arise as kings of the Lord. The Mantle of David is being released. We are to press on to the mark of our high calling. If we as a co-operate Church in revival over two years of revival, can find the level of miracles, signs and wonders. We can climb to the higher realm of Glory.

God is talking about the type of anointing that He is pouring upon the Church is Kingly oil. God says there are notable remarkable miracles coming. We will operate in healing like we have never before.

One time God showed me and said that we are to have extreme faith, such as hearing God say call the three worst cases up and give a promise they will be healed right then.

God said I'm about to move the Church to,
Acts 5:12-16 And by the hands of the apostles were many signs and wonders wrought

among the people; (and they were all with one accord in Solomon's porch. And of the rest durst no man join himself to them: but the people magnified them. And believers were the more added to the Lord, multitudes both of men and women.) Insomuch that they brought forth the sick into the streets, and laid *them* on beds and couches, that at the least the shadow of Peter passing by might overshadow some of them. There came also a multitude *out* of the cities round about unto Jerusalem, bringing sick folks, and them which were vexed with unclean spirits: and they were healed every one.

The atmosphere of God is going to begin to heal the multitude. The battling and testing is coming to an end.

I want to talk about David. It took him thirteen years for fullness. As soon as David was anointed king, He was king in the spirit. It was thirteen years for fullness in the natural to come.

Thirteen years of battle and then he was in Zion for thirty three years as king. The battle comes and the breaker anointing comes to break through new ground. (We will go in depth of the breaker anointing later in the book.) There are people in the battle now but if you receive this you will make it to where you're going. When the kingly anointing comes everything changes.

2 Samuel 5:1-4 Then came all the tribes of Israel to David unto Hebron, and spake, saying, Behold, we *are* thy bone and thy flesh. Also in time past, when Saul was king over us, thou wast he that leddest out and broughtest in Israel: and the LORD said to thee, Thou shalt feed my people Israel, and thou shalt be a captain over Israel. So all the elders of Israel came to the king to Hebron; and king David made a league with them in Hebron before the LORD: and they anointed David king over Israel. David *was* thirty years old when he began to reign, *and* he reigned forty years.

Up to this point David was in the wilderness and the battle. To get to where God has called you, we must fight our way there. We have broken ground but we need to break more ground. When we break through there is more and more to break through. Kings make it happen. I'm tired of just hearing about it. I want to do what God intends for us.

2 Samuel 5:4 David *was* thirty years old when he began to reign, *and* he reigned forty years.

40 years. 33 years over all of Israel.

2 Samuel 5:17 But when the Philistines heard that they had anointed David king over Israel, all the Philistines came up to seek David; and David heard *of it,* and went down to the hold.

This anointing will not come with out resistance.

2 Samuel 5:18 The Philistines also came and spread themselves in the valley of Rephaim.

David went to the place called breakthrough. There is a place called breakthrough in the Spirit.

When the anointing for breaking open we will break out of where we are. Jesus is the one who comes up before us. When this anointing comes you can't stay where you are. You are about to break out. If we can go to the place called breakthrough in the Spirit and touch it. This anointing will take off the caps and the limits.

2 Samuel 5:22 And the Philistines came up yet again, and spread themselves in the valley of Rephaim.

Are you ready to advance quickly? We have to respond quickly. Angelic Hosts for breakthrough are being released. The angel called breakthrough is ready. God showed me a warrior angel that was being released. His name is called breakthrough. The Holy Spirit releases us into the realm where we need to go. We are to bust open into the level of anointing. We need kingly anointing and Kingly oil.

THE REVELATORY ANOINTING

I ministered for years without this anointing and I don't know how I survived. Through this Chapter, I want to show you how to stir up the spirit of wisdom and revelation that the scripture refers to in Revelation 4. It's time that we, as the church, take back our inheritance, our call to see into the spiritual realm and live as supernatural beings living in a physical body. In order to walk into this inheritance, we need to be set free from the fear of deception which plagues so much of the church. When we have a biblical foundation for our lives and we see how naturally God's people have lived in the supernatural realm from the beginning to the end of the Bible, we can rest in the knowledge that such experiences are good gifts from the Father.

Yes, we need to lay out some guidelines through practical teaching on the do's and don'ts of experiencing the supernatural and handling revelation that is what I intend to do in this Chapter.

It is my prayer that this teaching will stir up revelation knowledge in you: word of knowledge, visions, and the whole prophetic realm. Do you want an increase of the prophetic in your life so you can hear God's voice clearer and increasingly experience wonderful encounters with the Holy Spirit? If so, then today is your day for flying higher in the supernatural realm. The first thing you need to understand is that true divine revelation is available in abundance and it's available to you! You need to understand how easy it is to receive revelation so you can grow in faith. God wants you to have great expectations of how much spiritual knowledge we can receive now if we will just learn to receive from Him. My desire is to raise the level of your expectation that God will speak to you and that He will give you supernatural revelation if you open your spirit to Him by faith.

We can truly trust Him to bless us with revelation because scripture tells us that if we ask for a good gift He won't give us something harmful, God is in the business of giving good things to those who ask Him.

Matthew 7:10, 11 Or if he ask a fish, will he give him a serpent? If ye then, being evil, know how to give good gifts unto your children, how much more shall your Father which is in heaven give good things to them that ask him?

The greatest of those good gifts the Father wants to give us is relationship with Him, which involves communication and hearing His voice. Remember, as believers, we have the Holy Spirit living inside of us. Scripture tells us in 1 Corinthians 2 that the Spirit searches all things, even the deep things of God He searches the mind of Christ. Consequently, because I have the Holy Spirit in me, anywhere I am, at any moment, I have access to the thoughts and the mind of Christ. I can also access the deep things of God through the Spirit in me who will bring revelation and searches all things.

When I saw this truth and started to lift my faith and expectation that I could be used in the prophetic and that I could hear God's voice, revelation from heaven began to increase. However, let me point out here that many of you may have heard God's voice and even prophesied, maybe a little on Sunday or a little song of the Lord here and there you've had the inspiration, the unction and the leading of the Spirit. But that's not the realm I'm talking about; I am talking about the extreme level of the prophetic visitations of angels, trances, visions and visits into the third heaven. I believe God wants to speak in these ways as well as through promptings and the still small voice.

When I began to see in scripture how natural these experiences were, I realized that I could also have trances like Peter; that I, like the apostle Paul, could go into paradise; and that I, like Ezekiel, could be taken by the Spirit into visions of God.

I started expecting, not just the prophetic, the still small voice, the little divine thoughts, or the body impressions of other people's pains or sicknesses. My faith started growing for experiencing God in a whole new realm, a realm of supernatural revelation common for those walking in the seer anointing. I started to believe that I could have a seer anointing like Elisha. The bible illustrates that this anointing can be received in prayer consider the story of Elisha praying for his servant, Gehazi, that the eyes of his heart could be opened to see into the second heaven (the realm of angels of demons). So I stretched my faith, to believe for a whole new dimension of the prophetic praying in faith became easy when I realized that revelation is available in abundance through the Holy Spirit inside me. So, anywhere I am, it is as easy as tuning into the Spirit of God within me to receive revelation from heaven.

The Bible says that God's thoughts toward us are precious and as innumerable as the sand of the sea.

Psalms 139:17, 18 How precious also are thy thoughts unto me, O God! how great is the sum of them! *If* I should count them, they are more in number than the sand: when I awake, I am still with thee.

God doesn't just have one thought toward us, but thoughts are countless. I believe that God wants to share those thoughts with us because, by His Spirit, He has given us the mind of Christ. Sometimes revelation from God is as easy as asking for just one thought that's all it takes to move in the prophetic.

Revelations 4:1 After this I looked, and, behold, a door *was* opened in heaven: and the first voice which I heard *was* as it were of a trumpet talking with me; which said, Come up hither, and I will shew thee things which must be hereafter.

So if heaven is going to touch earth with miracles, healings, signs, wonders, visions and revelation, heaven must be opened up for us. It was when heaven opened that John the apostle began to receive revelation.

Revelations 19:11 And I saw heaven opened, and behold a white horse; and he that sat upon him *was* called Faithful and True, and in righteousness he doth judge and make war.

As the church, we need to pray for an open heaven because that's what causes the prophetic to be released. In Revelation 4:1 a door is standing open in heaven and there comes an invitation: "Come up here, and I will show you things which must take place after this." I believe that John received revelation because that heavenly door never closed. And that door is still standing open in heaven today. As in Jacob's vision of the ladder going into heaven with the angels ascending and descending, those heavenly beings are still going into heaven and coming out with revelation from God.

Jacob's ladder, I believe, is still available to us today, to enable us to come into the spirit just like John, we can say, "immediately, I was in the spirit."

By faith we need to raise our expectation levels of how much we believe we can have now. I believe there is a door standing open in heaven and that we are invited to "Come up here!" When I saw that this same invitation was for me, I began to say, "Holy Spirit come, I'm climbing up that ladder. I'm going into the heavens; I'm getting revelation and bringing it out into the earth." Many of us don't experience this realm and dimension of the prophetic because we never put our faith out there for it. We might reach for a little prophecy but we never reach for angels or trances.

Revelations 4:6 And before the throne *there was* a sea of glass like unto crystal: and in the midst of the throne, and round about the throne, *were* four beasts full of eyes before and behind.

Have you ever wondered about the significance of the creatures full of eyes and of the crystal sea?

God said, "You are in the sea of revelation, you are in the sea of glass." The transparency spoke of how everything is transparent before God's throne and nothing can be hidden. Because He is the Alpha and Omega, He knows the Beginning and the End.

He knows the thoughts and hearts of every man and every woman who has ever lived. God is taking His church deeper in revelation, for the knowledge of the glory of the Lord will cover the earth as the water covers the sea. Then the Lord showed me that the eyes represented His all-knowing, all-seeing ability. Ezekiel 10 also refers to these eyes. However, this passage describes cherubim, full of eyes, moving with God's glory. Whenever the glory of the Lord moved with the Ark of the Covenant, the cherubim would move in the same direction. The eyes (the revelation) could be found everywhere the glory presence of the Lord went. We need to understand that heaven is full of revelation and that revelation is available to us, His children.

When you come into God's presence, it's like coming into the sea of glass or that place in heaven where all the eyes are. God wants to release that revelation knowledge to you today.

Besides the crystal sea and the eyes, scripture uses another symbol.

1 Samuel 14:29 Then said Jonathan, My father hath troubled the land: see, I pray you, how mine eyes have been enlightened, because I tasted a little of this honey.

I believe honey, here and throughout scripture, is a prophetic picture of revelation. When Jonathan took that honey and he tasted it, it brightened his countenance, quickened his understanding and made him sharp. That is what happens when you get into revelation it makes you quick and sharp. This is often the case for prophetic people.

Revelation supernaturally transforms your imagination and understanding. Revelation actually does something to your physical body; it actually does something to your mind. Perhaps you're saying today, "That is what I need. Give me a little of that spirit of wisdom and revelation."

We need to recognize that revelation comes from the Holy Ghost. Remember Jesus' words to Peter after he said that Jesus was the Son of God: "Flesh and blood has not revealed this to you but my Father who is in heaven." Yes, the Father has sent the Holy Spirit to give us revelation He lives inside each born-again believer. Also, it's important to know that revelation can be connected to a geographic place. I have been to regions of the earth where I experienced heightened revelation just because of where I was geographically I was in a place under a greater open heaven.

Genesis 28:10 And Jacob went out from Beersheba, and went toward Haran.

He went to a certain place.

Genesis 28:12 And he dreamed, and behold a ladder set up on the earth, and the top of it reached to heaven: and behold the angels of God ascending and descending on it.

I have also been to places where revelation was connected to the geographic location.

Some of us can't dream because of the spiritual atmosphere around us. That's why we need to learn the keys to opening heaven, so we can live and walk under an open heaven wherever we go. That's covered more in another message.

Atmosphere has everything to do with revelation. In scripture, when the minstrel played, the hand of the Lord came. God's throne on earth begins to be established when we worship. The seraphim angels in Revelation 4 worshipped 24 hours a day, night and day saying, "Holy, Holy, Holy, Lord God Almighty, who was and is and is to come!"

In that atmosphere of worship, we become transparent before God and He gives us eyes to see into the spirit realm. As we worship, God's glory presence becomes tangible and the creatures that cover and protect the cherubim and seraphim begin to be activated. As we worship together, God begins to change the atmosphere so that revelation can be released. When the minstrel plays, the hand of the Lord comes. So, I believe that there are atmospheres connected to geographical locations that make it easier for us to ascend into the heavens and return to earth with revelation.

As I continue to teach on the spirit of wisdom and revelation, I believe God wants to give you a powerful impartation from heaven. As you open your spirit right now, you can begin to receive down loads from the spirit. So you go ahead and have visions, trances, dreams or go to heaven any time that you want to. I expect you to see.

Ephesians 1:17 That the God of our Lord Jesus Christ, the Father of glory, may give unto you the spirit of wisdom and revelation in the knowledge of him:

I pray that the God of our Lord Jesus Christ, the Father of Glory, may give to you the spirit of wisdom and revelation in the knowledge of Him."

As this scripture shows us, wisdom and revelation is always connected to the knowledge of Him. This "knowledge of Him" is not knowledge about God. It's not the knowledge of scripture. It's not the knowledge of who God is and what He does. It's not the knowledge of theology and principles. This passage speaks of knowing Him through experience and intimacy because we have taken the time to be in His presence and we've taken the time to know Him, His ways, His heart and His character. God is calling us to receive the knowledge that only comes through experience because we have been at his feet.

The more we grow in the knowledge of Him, the more the spirit of wisdom and revelation will increase in our life.

God wants to give us the ministry of Jesus, which is the ministry of revelation.

Isaiah 11:2 And the spirit of the LORD shall rest upon him, the spirit of wisdom and understanding, the spirit of counsel and might, the spirit of knowledge and of the fear of the LORD;

These aspects of God's nature all go together. The Spirit of the Lord rests on Jesus wisdom and understanding as well as counsel which bring might and revelation which brings power!

Jesus said He only did those things He saw His Father doing. So the revelation what He saw the Father doing by vision He went and did in the earth. This combination of revelation, faith and obedience is what brought the power. I believe the passage in Isaiah shows us that counsel brings might these two spirits and natures of the Lord work together. Some of you don't have more might in your life because you don't have counsel in your life, because you're not tapping into God's heart and mind by stirring up the spirit of wisdom and revelation. Or perhaps you just haven't had the faith and expectation that this kind of prophetic is for you. You may have thought it was for the prophet, but not for you. However, God wants powerful revelation from heaven to become a common and everyday release in the body of Christ. We need to take the spookiness out of it trances, dreams and heavenly visitations need to become natural and common in the body of Christ because that is what the ministry of Jesus was. The ministry of Jesus was wisdom, understanding, counsel, might, knowledge and the fear of the Lord.

Ephesians 1:17, 18 That the God of our Lord Jesus Christ, the Father of glory, may give unto you the spirit of wisdom and revelation in the knowledge of him: The eyes of your understanding being enlightened; that ye may know what is the hope of his calling, and what the riches of the glory of his inheritance in the saints, It's extremely important that we have wisdom and revelation in our lives because only then will we have the rest of what Paul talks about. That is what revelation it brings a revelation of God's call and a sense of His purpose and destiny for your life. Without revelation we don't have that fire in our spirit, that desire, that love of Christ that constrains us or that fire that motivates moves and compels us. We need that passion inside us that says, "this is who I am and this is what I am going to do." This passion only comes out of revelation.

God also wants the eyes of our heart to be open so we can also understand what are "the riches of the glory of His inheritance in the saints, and what is the exceeding greatness of His power toward us who believe, according to the working of His mighty power which He worked in Christ when He raised Him from the Dead." Yes, the spirit of wisdom and revelation, as well as having the eyes of our heart enlightened, brings us into the manifestation of God's power. Without the revelation, we won't have a manifestation of

Gods' power because revelation is connected to the power of God, to miracles, signs and wonders. Revelation is always connected to raising the dead.

So where is this power? Is it in your life? Where is the manifestation of the exceeding greatness of His power? Somewhere along the line, the penny hasn't dropped. Somewhere along the line, we really haven't had revelation; we've only had knowledge. However, when the revelation happens, the manifestation happens and the demonstration happens. That is how Elijah operated. Think about Mt. Carmel and the great things that happened when he overcame the 450 prophets of Baal and the whole nation was turned back to God. We need to recognize that they had revival and reformation on that mountain. Fire came down from heaven signs and wonders were displayed. And how did all this happen?

1 Kings 18:36 And it came to pass at *the time of* the offering of the *evening* sacrifice, that Elijah the prophet came near, and said, LORD God of Abraham, Isaac, and of Israel, let it be known this day that thou *art* God in Israel, and

that I *am* thy servant, and *that* **I have done all these things at thy word**.

That was the secret to the power of God doing everything according to God's word. If we would have eyes to see and ears to hear under the spirit of wisdom and revelation, we would operate in the exceeding greatness of His power because the spirit of counsel always works with the spirit of might. As we ascend into heaven and we get revelation, we bring the manifestation to earth.

Do you know what revelation is? The word revelation means to reveal and disclose it is the secrets of the Lord. Revelation means appearing; it speaks of lightning; it means "the coming" and "the manifestation." Manifestation brings the revelation into the natural realm. We desperately need to have an increase of the spirit of wisdom and revelation. You know what wisdom is. Wisdom involves correct delivery and it means to rightly divide knowledge. When we receive God's wisdom, we know when and how to present our revelation to others in Christ's body.

As the Lord discloses the secrets of His heart to us faith rises in our hearts to see these spiritual things become a natural reality. If we don't have a revelation of the exceeding greatness of His power, we won't have the manifestation of the exceeding greatness of His power.

So how do we cultivate the lifestyle of receiving wisdom and revelation? Now, from a passage in 2 Peter, I am going to share with you some ways that you can stir up, and practically increase, the spirit of wisdom and revelation in your life.

2 Peter 1:2, 3 Grace and peace be multiplied unto you through the knowledge of God, and of Jesus our Lord, According as his divine power hath given unto us all things that *pertain* unto life and godliness, through the knowledge of him that hath called us to glory and virtue:

Intimacy: Notice that the first thing about revelation is that it is always connected to intimate knowledge of Him.

According to verse three, God has given us his divine power for everything pertaining to life, to divine power and to activating the provision of everything that we need to live a life of godliness it's all connected to the intimate knowledge of Him. All these treasures come from acquaintance with Him through prayer, intimacy, and worship, sitting as feet and being in His presence. As a result, the manifestation of His divine power comes automatically to give us everything we need to be as godly as God has called us to be. God has already made the provision; we just receive it through growing in intimate knowledge of Him.

Now, look at verse two: "Grace and peace be multiplied to you." How many of you would like the multiplication of grace and peace in your life? Again we see these blessings automatically poured into our lives in intimacy with Jesus. This grace is the divine influence or the evidence of God on the heart as well as the gift, favor and benefits of God. Wouldn't you like more of the favor of God, His divine benefits and supernatural influence in your life?

When that grace is multiplied, God's power is manifest on your life as well. It automatically takes place in intimacy isn't that awesome!

Peace is also a fruit of intimacy. The word peace means quietness, rest, prosperity and wholeness. How would you like the multiplication of this great peace that passes understanding? More Lord! As these wonderful blessings of grace and peace come on our lives in intimacy, we have more prosperity, quietness, rest, health and wholeness. The Father wants to give us everything we need for an abundant, godly life.

Verse four tells us that we can become a partaker of the divine nature of God. We partake through the exceeding great and precious promises, promises that have opened the door to fellowship, communion, partnership and association with God's divine nature, the very substance and character of who God and who Christ is. The character of God is locked up in the spirit of wisdom and in the spirit of revelation.

As we grow in revelation of the exceeding great and precious promises of God's word, an impartation of the divine nature of God comes automatically. When we flow in the prophetic anointing, the very divine nature, character, spirit and personality of Christ is imparted to us in intimacy through revelation. We will find people saying to us, "Wow, you do have more benefits; you do have more favor and you do have more power in your life. Why are you so blessed? You have more wholeness, more prosperity, more shalom, more quietness and more rest in your life." Then we can tell them that it's all connected to being intimately connected with Him. We become more like Him just because we are having revelation of the exceeding great and precious promises of God's word!

Meditation: The second thing that stirs up wisdom and revelation in our life is receiving the rhema promise of God through meditation.

2 Peter 1:19 We have also a more sure word of prophecy; whereunto ye do well that ye take heed, as unto a light that shineth in a dark place, until the day dawn, and the day star arise in your hearts:

This scripture refers to the prophetic word, the rhema word or the word the Father speaks personally to our hearts. God's word is like a light that shines in a dark place. That's how revelation starts God's word shines brightly in dark places in us till the day dawns and the morning star rises in our heart.

So how do we convert that shining inner word into transforming revelation? "Through meditation." Here's how the Lord has taught me to meditate on Scripture. I take God's word or promise and begin to read over it, allowing that light to shine in my heart. As I continue to meditate on the scripture and confess it, pray it, read it, think about it and contemplate day and night, it comes as a light within my heart. And through that process of meditation upon that word, it begins to rise and fill my heart; it begins to rise as the sun at the dawning of a new day.

God's rhema, prophetic spoken word to us is always like a light shining in the dark. But as we begin to understand the light of God's word, His word is a lamp to our feet. This is how you partake of the exceeding greatness of His precious promises.

Meditation and revelation are interconnected meditation brings revelation and revelation brings the manifestation of what has been revealed. When we first see or hear the word, it's really not revealed because it is only a light that shines in our heart. However, when we meditate on it and when we pray it, revelation comes and begins working to bring the manifestation and the experience. So why don't we often have the manifestation of what we know? Because we really haven't meditated on those words from the Lord till we received that blazing revelation inside that would release the manifestation of the promise. We need to read and speak out those scriptures and promises over and over again. We've got to say that scripture repeatedly and meditate on a single verse for thirty minutes or more. It will open up like the drawing of a dark curtain and the Son's light will come on!

So the second key to stirring up the spirit of wisdom and revelation is receiving the rhema promise through meditation.

Godly Character: Another key to stirring up wisdom and revelation is godly character.

2 Peter 1:5-9 And beside this, giving all diligence, add to your faith virtue; and to virtue knowledge; And to knowledge temperance; and to temperance patience; and to patience godliness; And to godliness brotherly kindness; and to brotherly kindness charity.

For if these things be in you, and abound, they make *you that ye shall* neither *be* barren nor unfruitful in the knowledge of our Lord Jesus Christ. But he that lacketh these things is blind, and cannot see afar off, and hath forgotten that he was purged from his old sins.

There is a connection between partaking of the divine nature and character. We begin to long to be more like Jesus: "Lord, I want to be like you.

Let me behold you, for I can only become like the one I see. I know I can't really become who you want me to be until I've been in your presence because I become what I see." So as we begin to behold the glory of the Only Begotten Son, as we begin to fix and turn our eyes upon Jesus, as we begin to gaze upon His face and as we begin to spend time in His presence, His character and very nature begins to be forged in us. Godly character continues to grow as we yield ourselves to the Holy Spirit's cleansing process and as we submit to the discipline of the Father. Our hearts need to cry out for the Spirit of God to change us.

As we love who God is and love His character being worked in us, we are saying: "Holy Spirit help me. I can't do it without you, because I only become what I see. So as I see you, there is a transference that takes place by the Spirit of God to transform us from glory to glory." When our heart cries out like that, the Spirit brings us into an increase of the Spirit of wisdom and revelation because the Bible says that if these things are yours and abound in us, we will not be barren or unfruitful.

Some of you are barren and unfruitful in revelation in your life because of character. On the other hand, some of you are barren and unfruitful in your life because you have an empty well. You can't have revelation if the well is empty, if you haven't been meditating on God's word day and night. Only as you meditate, and live in intimacy, will you partake of the exceeding great and precious promises as well as His divine nature and character! When you don't partake of God's nature, then you are not fruitful in revelation and you are short sighted or even blind.

We can't become who God wants us to be without partaking of Him, without the grace, without the divine influence. And the divine influence doesn't happen if we are not in the knowledge of Him. If we are not intimately connected to Him, there isn't the process of the multiplication of the grace, peace and divine influence on our lives to become who He wants us to be. Out of that divine influence, comes everything pertaining to life. Life! God's blessing begins to be poured out on our finances, family, business and physical health all things.

See the whole process is woven together. God has put His divine nature in the prophetic word. In that word will release character growth. A passion to grow in Christ like character is vitally connected to growing in wisdom and revelation. Take time to meditate on the first eight verses of 2 Peter chapter 1 until you get the wonderful revelation in this passage.

Waiting for God's Counsel: this is the fourth key to stirring up the spirit of wisdom.

Psalms 106:13 They soon forgat his works; they waited not for his counsel:

Psalms 106:15 And he gave them their request; but sent leanness into their soul.

1 Samuel 3:1 And the child Samuel ministered unto the LORD before Eli. And the word of the LORD was precious in those days; *there was* no open vision.

Are you in a place where the word of the Lord is rare in your life? Are you in a place where visions are infrequent and you're lacking prophetic vision?

The increase of revelation comes as we wait for His counsel. Revelation was rare to the people of Israel because they weren't taking time to wait in His presence expecting to hear from Him. We need to come to Him saying, "Here I am Lord, an hour before the service tonight, to get counsel of what you want me to do before I do it." Jesus wants us to only do those things that we see the Father doing He doesn't want us doing things just because of traditions or because of man's ideas. I believe Jesus saw what the Father was doing in the place of waiting He would get up a long while before day to pray and He would wait on the mountain all night. That's where he would get the open vision to see what the Father did so He could go out and do it that day. Jesus received that counsel and revelation because He often withdrew into the wilderness and prayed. And it wasn't just about praying. I believe He had times when He sat at the Father's feet, like Mary sat at His feet, and He didn't say anything. He just looked up at the face of God waiting, waiting, waiting, waiting, and waiting.

Maybe you don't wait.

I got the word of knowledge flowing in my life waiting on God and being faithful, with what He gave me. The more I waited, the more God gave me details about what was wrong with people's bodies. I would take the time on a daily basis, not to pray, but to lie on the carpet, be in His presence, and wait. "What do you want to do tonight Father?" And the next day, "What do you want to do tonight Father?" Pastors often start that way... and then they get busy. I have waited, at times 1-3 hours a day, everyday in silence for a revelation and for visions.

There was a time in my life when God in His sovereignty visited me for months, hours a day all I did was lie on the floor and wait for counsel, for wisdom and for revelation. I would just lie in His presence and wait until I would see. As I faithfully did that on a daily basis,

God increased the spirit of wisdom and revelation in my life. I'm not talking about being in the word or being in prayer I'm talking about the place in God's presence where you don't do anything but wait.

As we learn to wait on the Lord, the wasting disease and leanness of soul is replaced with revelation, fruitfulness, favor and financial prosperity. As we spend time waiting before the Lord, He opens up the television screen in heaven for us to see what the Father is doing.

Sanctified Imagination: If we want to see in the spirit, we must use the powerful key of sanctified imagination to unlock visions and dreams. What do you think about when preachers say, "I saw in the spirit?" Often, we automatically think they saw with their natural eyes. I have helped bring so many people into the heavenly realm by teaching them to look with their spiritual eye and to stop asking, "Where is it? Where is the angel? Where? I don't see him where?" We have to begin to see with the eye on the inside, in our imagination. I showed you this eye in Ephesians 1 it is called the "eyes of your understanding." You don't see spiritual things with natural eyes; you see them with the eyes of your heart, your spiritual eyes! I believe that most of all visions and revelations happen in the eye of our hearts, in our imagination. Think of how we daydream. We may be at work, but we see ourselves on the beach. That's where visions happen in that same realm, the place of the daydream. However, in this case, God initiates the daydreams. Here's how sanctified daydreaming happens. You're not thinking about anything you're just waiting on the Lord, asking the Holy Spirit to come when God initiates a prophetic daydream. There is such a connection between our thoughts and God's thoughts. That's why we need to sanctify the imagination. So we need to understand that we aren't to look with these eyes, we are to look on the inside.

When people are looking at the screen of our imagination, sometimes I hear them say: "Wait a minute! I think I just saw something. But maybe it was just me, or maybe it was God, or maybe I am just thinking that." Well, so what! Let me ask you a question. If it's not direction and it's not going to alter your life or anybody else's, what is the problem? Perhaps you see yourself riding on a horse with Jesus. What if it was really just you thinking that? My question to you is: "How did that picture make you feel?" if you're lying on the carpet saying, "Holy Spirit come and sanctify my imagination; I want to be with Jesus in the spirit" and you suddenly go into some kind of prophetic daydream, you just could be having a heavenly experience. You know how I know that? Remember, even Paul the Apostle, when he had his experience in paradise, as grand as it was, said, "Whether in the body.... or whether out of the body I do not know." So even Paul wasn't sure whether he actually physically traveled or whether he was just in paradise in spirit. Paul didn't know, so don't you worry about figuring out all your experiences. The more we learn to sanctify the imagination, the more we will experience revelation from the Lord.

You've got to seek wisdom: God talks about wisdom and revelation using the personal pronoun "her". To get wisdom, you've got to seek, love and honor her. You've got to promote her. You've got to want her and make yourself available for her. I pursue wisdom on a daily basis. When I got saved I prayed everyday for the Spirit of wisdom.

Everyday I spent hours looking for revelation; it became a part of me because it's a part of

Jesus. Let's learn more about this highly prized wisdom:

Proverbs 2:1, 2 My son, if thou wilt receive my words, and hide my commandments with thee; So that thou incline thine ear unto wisdom, *and* apply thine heart to understanding;
The Lord wants us lift our voice and cry out for understanding. He wants us to "seek her as silver, and search for her as for hidden treasures" then we will "understand the fear of the Lord, and find the knowledge of God." For the Lord gives wisdom, knowledge and understanding to the upright.

Proverbs 4:5 Get wisdom, get understanding: forget *it* not; neither decline from the words of my mouth.

Do you want an increase of the spirit of wisdom and revelation?

Let's begin to follow Solomon's instructions and begin to prayerfully seek for these treasures, searching for the Spirit of Wisdom! Holy Spirit come!

Isaiah 11:2 And the spirit of the LORD shall rest upon him, the spirit of wisdom and understanding, the spirit of counsel and might, the spirit of knowledge and of the fear of the LORD;

Come on, I want you to continue seeking her. You may not have ever done it like this before; so let's learn together. Let's continue to pray and cry out for discernment.

GIFT OF THE ANOINTING

God gives gifts to men and women whom are available to be used. In this Chapter I want to lay some simple scriptures for you to receive. This is a precious time of the Lord pouring out His spirit.

Ephesians 4:7 But unto every one of us is given grace according to the measure of the gift of Christ.

Ephesians 4:11, 12 And he gave some, apostles; and some, prophets; and some, evangelists; and some, pastors and teachers; For the perfecting of the saints, for the work of the ministry, for the edifying of the body of Christ:

Allot of people have gifts but they are for them. Not the equipping of the Saints.

Ephesians 4:13 Till we all come in the unity of the faith, and of the knowledge of the Son of

God, unto a perfect man, unto the measure of the stature of the fulness of Christ:

There will come a day that anyone that is a believer will flow in gifts like Jesus did. The Spirit of God is about to move and there will become a nameless faceless generation.

Romans 12:3-8 For I say, through the grace given unto me, to every man that is among you, not to think *of himself* more highly than he ought to think; but to think soberly, according as God hath dealt to every man the measure of faith. For as we have many members in one body, and all members have not the same office: So we, *being* many, are one body in Christ, and every one members one of another. Having then gifts differing according to the grace that is given to us, whether prophecy, *let us prophesy* according to the proportion of faith; Or ministry, *let us wait* on *our* ministering: or he that teacheth, on teaching; Or he that exhorteth, on exhortation: he that giveth, *let him do it* with simplicity; he that ruleth, with diligence; he that sheweth mercy, with cheerfulness. There are measures of faith. We can build our faith up. We will go into more detail in the last Chapter.

THE BREAKER ANOINTING

If you have ever been at a place you couldn't break through, this is for you. The Breaker Anointing I will share exciting revelations that will not only encourage your faith to soar; they will also inspire you to overcome impossible looking situations so that you get the breakthroughs that God intends. In this hour, more than ever before, there is a bigger dimension of God's authority in the anointing to break through! I saw by the spirit "The breaker anointing" began to operate and hundreds of us saw breakthroughs actually happen! If such breakthroughs could happen like that before, then they can happen again; even more so!

Therefore it's so on my heart to declare, today, that we need to be vigilant, right now, about pressing in for the breaker anointing for breakthroughs.

I am carrying that anointing right now. I believe what happened in Litchfield will become normal Christianity. I also believe it was a small measure compared to what is coming. Every believer will be having encounters like you read about in the book of Acts.

I have been prophesying for several years now that all young men will have visions and all old men will dream dreams.

Acts 2:17 And it shall come to pass in the last days, saith God, I will pour out of my Spirit upon all flesh: and your sons and your daughters shall prophesy, and your young men shall see visions, and your old men shall dream dreams:

In other words there will be a place in the church where dreams and visions will be common for every believer! I believe also that God's direction will come to us by way of the angel of the Lord.

Just like the angel supernaturally released the apostles from prison, led them out and then told them what to do next, I believe intervention like this will happen again in our day.

Acts 5:19, 20 But the angel of the Lord by night opened the prison doors, and brought them forth, and said, Go, stand and speak in the temple to the people all the words of this life.

Look at what happened to Peter when he was chained up in jail another time.

Acts 12:5-16 Peter therefore was kept in prison: but prayer was made without ceasing of the church unto God for him. And when Herod would have brought him forth, the same night Peter was sleeping between two soldiers, bound with two chains: and the keepers before the door kept the prison. And, behold, the angel of the Lord came upon *him,* and a light shined in the prison: and he smote Peter on the side, and raised him up, saying, Arise up quickly. And his chains fell off from *his* hands. And the angel said unto him, Gird thyself, and bind on thy sandals. And so he did. And he saith unto him, Cast thy garment about thee, and follow me. And he went out, and followed him; and wist not that it was true which was done by the angel; but thought he saw a vision. When they were past the first and the second ward, they came unto the iron gate that leadeth unto the city; which opened to them of his own accord: and they went out, and passed on through one street; and forthwith the angel departed from him. And when Peter was come to himself, he said, Now I know of a surety, that the Lord hath sent his angel, and hath delivered me out of the hand of Herod, and *from* all the expectation of the people of the Jews. And when he had considered *the thing,* he came to the house of Mary the mother of John, whose surname was Mark; where many were gathered together praying. And as Peter knocked at the door of the gate, a damsel came to hearken, named Rhoda. And when she knew Peter's voice, she opened not the gate for gladness, but ran in, and told how Peter stood before the gate. And they said unto her, Thou art mad. But she constantly affirmed that it was even so. Then said they, It is his angel. But Peter continued knocking: and when they had opened *the door,* and saw him, they were astonished.

When the church was praying like crazy for him an angel appeared at night in his cell and poked him sharply, waking him up, saying, "Get up quickly!" When he did, his chains supernaturally fell off his hands! His guards must have been in a "deep" sleep! The angel told him what to do next and Peter followed that angel through the front gate, which just happened to open all by itself. After he walked down one street the angel left him and he ended up at that very prayer meeting where they were madly praying for him.

What a breakthrough those prayer warriors had! Are you getting excited? If God is for us, then who can be against us!?

Romans 8:31 What shall we then say to these things? If God *be* for us, who *can be* against us?

God might decide to send an angel to help us like he did for the apostles, or He might decide to come to our aid Himself, or both! King David discovered this.

Once when the Philistines learned that David was anointed king over Israel, they went up to search for him. David heard of it, so he went down to his stronghold while the enemy deployed themselves strategically. Then David inquired of the Lord, asking whether he should fight them and whether God would deliver them into his hand. Immediately the Lord told David to go up against them, "for I will doubtless deliver the Philistines into your hand."

2 Samuel 5:17-19 But when the Philistines heard that they had anointed David king over Israel, all the Philistines came up to seek David; and David heard *of it,* and went down to the hold. The Philistines also came and spread themselves in the valley of Rephaim. And David enquired of the LORD, saying, Shall I go up to the Philistines? wilt thou deliver them into mine hand? And the LORD said unto David, Go up: for I will doubtless deliver the Philistines into thine hand.

Now don't miss this! When David went up and defeated them, he declared: "The Lord has broken through my enemies before me, like a breakthrough of water"

2 Samuel 5:20 And David came to Baalperazim, and David smote them there, and said, The LORD hath broken forth upon mine enemies before me, as the breach of waters. Therefore he called the name of that place Baalperazim.

And then, you know what happened? The enemy returned another time!

2 Samuel 5:22 And the Philistines came up yet again, and spread themselves in the valley of Rephaim.

Once again David inquired of the Lord, and this time God gave him an unusual battle plan.

He said to circle around behind the enemy and come at them from the front of the balsam trees.

2 Samuel 5:23 And when David enquired of the LORD, he said, Thou shalt not go up; *but* fetch a compass behind them, and come upon them over against the mulberry trees.

God said to listen for the sound of marching in the tops of the mulberry trees and then advance quickly, for He was going to go out before them to strike the enemy.

2 Samuel 5:24 And let it be, when thou hearest the sound of a going in the tops of the mulberry trees, that then thou shalt bestir thyself: for then shall the LORD go out before thee, to smite the host of the Philistines.

The marching sound in the mulberry trees was the marching of the angelic hosts.

One of the words God is giving me in the spirit right now is "advance." There are doors of opportunity open before you, but you need to advance quickly. God is about to release His angelic hosts before us. All of a sudden, It will be like water, it will break out and go to the nations. It's like the blessing of the Lord is waiting for you, waiting to overtake you. So open the door and let it gush on you! Advance quickly when God tells you!

We breakthrough to advance and we breakthrough, or take ground in advance. What does it mean to breakthrough in advance? It means: to come before as a forerunner

Micah 2:13 The breaker is come up before them: they have broken up, and have passed through the gate, and are gone out by it: and their king shall pass before them, and the LORD on the head of them.

In other words, the one who breaks open will come up before them, like a forerunner and then they will break out. It's breaking in and breaking out.

Actually the ground that the forerunners break through and break into, in the spirit, is ground that you break out (into) as well. The forerunners break open the ground and take ground in the spirit and go up beforehand, it's so that other believers can break through later on. That's the anointing that God is releasing right now.

Then what happens? The church breaks out "pass through the gate, and go out by it; their king will pass before them, with the LORD at their head."

Simultaneously as the church breaks out, the church is pressing in.

Luke 16:16 The law and the prophets *were* until John: since that time the kingdom of God is preached, and every man presseth into it.

Now let's look at two points. First, the kingdom of God is the invisible realm around you. It's the realm of "on earth as it is in heaven."

Matthew 6:10 Thy kingdom come. Thy will be done in earth, as *it is* in heaven.

On the one hand you don't have a kingdom without a king and on the other hand one of the first signs of the kingdom is a King---which is Jesus.

Second, that realm of God's Spirit, the kingdom of God, doesn't come without pressing in. "The kingdom of God has been preached and everyone is pressing into it." It doesn't come without contending.

Pressing into it means that there is a passionate pursuit of God in prayer. There is a pressing in. That means there is a seeking. Some of us don't even know what it means to seek. Yet the Bible promises that if you seek for Him and search for Him with all of your heart then you will find Him.

Jeremiah 29:13 And ye shall seek me, and find *me,* when ye shall search for me with all your heart.

The word, seek means: to diligently look for and to search out earnestly until the object of the search is located.

It's not just seeking, it's earnestly seeking. It's passionate pursuit of God in prayer. It's pressing into the kingdom by keeping on! Keeping on asking, keeping on seeking, crying out and hungering for the presence. It's consistently seeking God!

My point is this: how desperate are you? How hungry are you?

Psalms 63:1 A Psalm of David, when he was in the wilderness of Judah. O God, thou *art* my God; early will I seek thee: my soul thirsteth for thee, my flesh longeth for thee in a dry and thirsty land, where no water is;

What is it about early? You have to be desperate to seek God early and consistently. This is a main key for pressing in and walking in the breaker anointing.

Don't give up! Many have died not receiving the promise.

Hebrews 11:13 These all died in faith, not having received the promises, but having seen them afar off, and were persuaded of *them,* and embraced *them,* and confessed that they were strangers and pilgrims on the earth.

Pressing in for breakthroughs is a "place of contending." I remember contending for healing. If I prayed for a hundred and nobody was healed I was ready to pray for another thousand. I was going for the breakthrough. I was going to break out, take ground, and make an advance to make room for the thousands to come in behind me to touch the realms that we are just beginning to touch.

Let's never be satisfied with what we've seen or where we've been. You can advance quickly right now because there is a sound in the spirit prophetically and it's the sound of the angelic hosts and they are marching, and there is a great opportunity, a window in time for you to make great advances in the kingdom.

There is permission where there was never permission before. Grace where there was never grace before. Countries and nations that were never open before will be opened; it's a short time in which the window is open.

Whenever commitment and a persevering spirit press in to the kingdom of God (that's being released), they are always met by resistance from the enemy. There's a demonic confrontation with real powers of hell and darkness. But we can actually bring the battle to the enemy's door. We don't need to wait for powers of darkness to come knocking at our door. We need to be prepared.

I hope you're getting hungry for the breaker anointing!

The Breaker Anointing is sure to topple any thoughts that Christianity is humdrum! You'll be on the edge of your seat as you discover how much it's on God's heart to empower you to totally rout the enemy by daring to operate in the breaker anointing. So get ready to come up higher and launch into the heart of God's purposes in these end days.

In heat of battle, the leader, the one in authority, gives the order to charge. We have such a leader the One Who has all authority. He is the Lord of Hosts, the King of glory. He is King of Kings, and one day He will break through from heaven to earth with the armies of heaven riding on white horses following Him into battle!

Revelations 19:14, 15 And the armies *which were* in heaven followed him upon white horses, clothed in fine linen, white and clean. And out of his mouth goeth a sharp sword, that with it he should smite the nations: and he shall rule them with a rod of iron: and he treadeth the winepress of the fierceness and wrath of Almighty God.

Psalms 24:8-10 Who *is* this King of glory? The LORD strong and mighty, the LORD mighty in battle. Lift up your heads, O ye gates; even lift *them* up, ye everlasting doors; and the King of glory shall come in. Who is this King of glory? The LORD of hosts, he *is* the King of glory. Selah.

One day we're going to be in God's heavenly army descending with Jesus into earth's atmosphere after the marriage supper of the Lamb. Although this is the ultimate breakthrough, you might be wondering what this has to do with the breaker anointing.

Well, by the time we're riding on those white steeds behind Jesus, our character will have been refined through many experiences. I have learned obedience to God's orders. In fact, right now friends, it is time to practice for our eternal reign with Christ by obeying God's orders now.

What does God want in this hour? He wants us to experience many different kinds of breakthroughs, And He wants us to break through and follow Him into the harvest fields. It's time to advance! And let's remember also that when we take the gospel into the nations, essentially we're taking the battle to the enemy's door. But God is with us, our Great Commander "The Lord mighty in battle"!

So God wants to equip us, and He wants to prepare us to win the battle by winning the lost to Him. A huge part of that equipping is learning to walk in the authority that He has given us. I want to repeat what I said last week, "In this hour, more than ever before, there is a bigger dimension of God's authority in the anointing to break through!"

Will we believe God and obey Him by taking up our authority in the anointing to break through? Let's not be negligent. After all, He's telling us it's time to advance. Ready, Set, Charge! "We need to learn how to break through in the nations."

But listen; seriously; even more than calling on people like the ambassador, it's time to call on our God and call down His fire to burn up works of darkness just like Elijah did!

1 Kings 18:37-40 Hear me, O LORD, hear me, that this people may know that thou *art* the LORD God, and *that* thou hast turned their heart back again. Then the fire of the LORD fell, and consumed the burnt sacrifice, and the wood, and the stones, and the dust, and licked up the water that *was* in the trench. And when all the people saw *it,* they fell on their faces: and they said, The LORD, he *is* the God; the LORD, he *is* the God. And Elijah said unto them, Take the prophets of Baal; let not one of them escape. And they took them: and Elijah brought them down to the brook Kishon, and slew them there.

You know, the spirit and power that was upon Elijah also rested upon John the Baptist.

Matthew 11:11, 12 Verily I say unto you, Among them that are born of women there hath not risen a greater than John the Baptist: notwithstanding he that is least in the kingdom of heaven is greater than he. And from the days of John the Baptist until now the kingdom of heaven suffereth violence, and the violent take it by force.

There is something about pressing into the kingdom with violence.

The word violent means: to seize, to take by force.

It's about a commitment to overcome and break through resistance and contend for breakthroughs with a passionate pursuit of God in prayer; a seeking of God's purposes. There has to be a burning fiery heart of evangelism if we are going to advance this gospel. There must be an aggressiveness that comes out of a burning heart like John the Baptist's.

John 5:35 He was a burning and a shining light: and ye were willing for a season to rejoice in his light.

We are not going to take cities and nations for God without a conviction, without a fire, without a burning heart of fiery witness and passion. "The violent take it by force."

The people with keen enthusiasm and commitment are willing to respond and propagate the gospel with radical abandonment. God is going to release that fire, that revival mantle again. The gospel is the power of God, not in word only, but in power. But this fact is often ignored.

Matthew 12:13-16 Then saith he to the man, Stretch forth thine hand. And he stretched *it* forth; and it was restored whole, like as the other. Then the Pharisees went out, and held a council against him, how they might destroy him. But when Jesus knew *it,* he withdrew himself from thence: and great multitudes followed him, and he healed them all; And charged them that they should not make him known:

He had just given this incredible illustration of advancing the gospel with a burning heart, with violence in the spirit, and being aggressive and diligent in pushing the gospel forward. He was talking about John the Baptist as the breaker that was sent before.

Yet Jesus was moved to say, "But this generation." "What shall I liken this generation?" He compared them like this:

Matthew 12:16, 17 And charged them that they should not make him known: That it might be fulfilled which was spoken by Esaias the prophet, saying,

You know what that means? They were non responsive. We have a church today that is non responsive. We are out of touch. We have lost passion. We are just laid back.

The Word says, the kingdom of heaven suffers violence and the violent take it by force but what shall I liken this generation? The people were not forceful at all. Again, likewise, our generation today is soft, weak, and non responsive. "Just wait for it to come; don't rock the boat; be careful." "I'm afraid to take it to the enemy. The devil is going to jump on me. Someone is going to reject me." Get over it. So what! If they kill you, what a greater martyr's blessing!

When the people went out to see John they thought they were going to see somebody who was weak and gentle.

That's what people expect to see in the church today something weak, soft, political, the same old 'don't rock the boat' stuff. They expect nice comfy pews. They don't want to have some guy yelling in their face, "Repent, for the kingdom of God is at hand!" Yet, some guy yelling "repent" just might be the one who breaks things open.

There are few people in the church today that really have the anointing to break through. That is why there are so many in the church that have vision but they never go anywhere. They have no breaker anointing. God wants to release the breaker anointing. It's an unprecedented time for asking and receiving in your heart nations!

Where you have never broken through before, where the doors have never opened before, where you have never found oil and favor before, where there has never been any permission before,

There is Permission Now!

It's time to advance! Don't stay where you are! Let God enlarge the vision in your heart. Lift up your eyes. We are talking about the breakthrough anointing. We need to learn how to contend for miracles. Come on. Let's contend in the spirit right now! Let your spirit press in right now! Push all the way through! Lift up your voice! Rip open the membrane!

Rip open the heavens right now!

Take ground! Breakthrough! New ground! New territories! New realms of authority! Breakthrough! Advancing! The angelic host is advancing! I hear the sound in the mulberry trees. God is breaking through! The Lord of the breakthrough! He is breaking through like the mighty waters pushing back demonic resistance, demonic powers of darkness. We get a breakthrough! Come on, God! We open heaven wide! Go through! Break out! Break out! Go through! Go through! Break out! Break out!

I want to break you through into a higher place of authority, a higher place of faith, a higher place of power! You tell God, "God, I climb into a new place of authority. I step into that realm and right now I grab hold of millions in the spirit, Lord. I step into the realm of millions of souls right now (for the harvest)." I push you through! God, I impart and I pray today, a real impartation of that fiery fervent spirit. God, release the anointing of the breaker; the anointing that breaks every yoke and removes every burden. In Jesus' name I pray. Amen.

THE MANIFESTED ANOINTING

God is causing such an increase of His anointing. He will cause a manifested anointing like never before. We will examine how having a God consciousness helps to us understand who we are and what we have available to us in our inheritance because we are children of God. We will discuss what it takes to be a people who manifest the anointing and those who dispense the glory of God in the earth. I will explain how God gives believers creative abilities and how our gifts and talents can reveal the Lord's heart to lost humanity and how we can tap into our creative abilities for the glory of God. As well, we will take a look at the scope of our authority and dominion in the earth and how the church can be a manifest expression of what Jesus looked liked 2,000 years ago. We will discover some practical keys that will release God's power and how the word of knowledge works to bring healing and deliverance in peoples lives.

Colossians 1:27 To whom God would make known what *is* the riches of the glory of this mystery among the Gentiles; which is Christ in you, the hope of glory:

God, we want to ask you for the spirit of wisdom and revelation in the knowledge of Him. Jesus, please give us a revelation of your presence, a revelation of your power. God, we want to know who you are, who we are and what we have. So God, I pray today to receive a much greater awareness of you. Thank you, in Jesus mighty name.

Before we examine how to manifest the anointing, we need to understand who we are and what we have available to us as an inheritance because we are sons and daughters of God. Three scriptures spoken by the apostle Paul in the Book of Romans in the 8th chapter lay a foundation concerning this.

Romans 8:2 For the law of the Spirit of life in Christ Jesus hath made me free from the law of sin and death.

Romans 8:15 For ye have not received the spirit of bondage again to fear; but ye have received the Spirit of adoption, whereby we cry, Abba, Father.

Romans 8:17 And if children, then heirs; heirs of God, and joint-heirs with Christ; if so be that we suffer with *him,* that we may be also glorified together.

We can see that we are children of God, heirs, set free from the law of sin and death and we have an inheritance in Christ. We need to come to understand who we are and what we have by developing a God consciousness. This awareness will give believers the first key they need to unlock God's power concerning manifesting the anointing.

Also, I believe that a time is coming when God will reveal and manifest His glory in us. So let's continue in the Book of Romans with more revelation by the apostle Paul.

Romans 8:18-23 For I reckon that the sufferings of this present time *are* not worthy *to be compared* with the glory which shall be revealed in us. For the earnest expectation of the creature waiteth for the manifestation of the sons of God. For the creature was made subject to vanity, not willingly, but by reason of him who hath subjected *the same* in hope, Because the creature itself also shall be delivered from the bondage of corruption into the glorious liberty of the children of God. For we know that the whole creation groaneth and travaileth in pain together until now. And not only *they,* but ourselves also, which have the firstfruits of the Spirit, even we ourselves groan within ourselves, waiting for the adoption, *to wit,* the redemption of our body.

Paul explains that creation itself and those who are gripped by sin (sickness, disease, death, and decay), long to be set free from sin's evil power. But before deliverance can come, the body of Christ needs a revelation of who we are and what we have.

We need to understand what it means to be set free from the law of sin and death, which is: sickness, disease, poverty and what it means to be joint heirs with an inheritance. This understanding and revelation is the revealing and the manifestation of the sons and daughters of God.

God wants to put inside our hearts the revelation of what it really means to be His sons and daughters. As believers, when we come into a greater understanding of this we will step into the kind of ministry that brings the earth and the world that's in corruption into what we call the glorious liberty of the children of God.? This glorious liberty means freedom from the law of sin, sickness, disease and death. And so there is a deliverance that is taking place in creation called the glorious liberty of the children of God? Where the sons and daughters of God are being revealed as they walk in the manifestation of the anointing. In fact, this is what it means to be ambassadors for Christ.

2 Corinthians 5:19, 20 To wit, that God was in Christ, reconciling the world unto himself, not imputing their trespasses unto them; and hath committed unto us the word of reconciliation. Now then we are ambassadors for Christ, as though God did beseech *you* by us: we pray *you* in Christ's stead, be ye reconciled to God.

Ambassadors have a job to do: set the captives free, break the curse of the law and expose, destroy the work of the devil. They help others come to understand the magnitude of their inheritance as sons and daughters who are adopted by the Father and those who are destined to manifest the anointing. Ambassadors for Christ don't want people to focus their attention on them, but rather that people would see and feel Jesus and His presence being released through them. God wants His sons and daughters to walk victoriously, triumphantly, conquering and overcoming the enemy. His desire is to see his children walking in God consciousness, possessing and manifesting the anointing like the apostles Peter, Paul, Moses and the prophet Elisha.

Jesus is the Son of God, who perfectly modeled the manifest anointing. His anointing for healing touched many people, sometimes through His personal laying on of hands, or when someone touched his clothing. And they begged Him that they might only touch the hem of His garment. And as many as touched it was made perfectly well.

Matthew 14:36 And besought him that they might only touch the hem of his garment: and as many as touched were made perfectly whole.

Power actually manifest on the clothes of Jesus and that's why, when the woman with the issue of blood touched the hem of his garment, she was healed.

Matthew 9:21, 22 For she said within herself, If I may but touch his garment, I shall be whole. But Jesus turned him about, and when he saw her, he said, Daughter, be of good comfort; thy faith hath made thee whole. And the woman was made whole from that hour.

He was carrying the power of the Lord which is present to heal because He was carrying substance on His life, the manifest anointing.

The apostle Peter was a son of God who possessed and understood the manifestation of the anointing. In Acts 5 we read how Peter carried such a great anointing that when people brought the sick on their beds and couches out onto the streets of Jerusalem, the shadow of Peter would heal their sicknesses. I'm not referring to the natural shadow of Peter, but rather to the same shadow that came upon Mary and overshadowed her with the power of the Most High when she conceived Jesus. It's the overshadowing of the presence and canopy of the Holy Spirit.

Also, the apostle Paul was another son of God who carried the manifestation of the anointing to such a great extent that God worked unusual miracles by his hands.

Acts 19:11 And God wrought special miracles by the hands of Paul:

Paul took the anointing and the substance that he possessed and put it on handkerchiefs or aprons and when the cloths were carried from his body to the sick and demonized, they were healed and set free because of the resident anointing on the material.

Acts 19:12 So that from his body were brought unto the sick handkerchiefs or aprons, and the diseases departed from them, and the evil spirits went out of them.

I don't believe the handkerchiefs or aprons were merely a point of contact. I believe that the substance of God the living, manifest, tangible, transferable anointing of the Holy Ghost that Paul carried was transferred to these cloths because they were in contact with the manifest presence of God on or in Paul's body. Scripture doesn't give details concerning the exact kind of contact the material had with his body, but it would be reasonable to imagine Paul laying hands on the material before it was carried to the sick.

The Bible doesn't give a lot of detail, but we feel that desperate family members of the sick and demonized brought handkerchiefs or aprons to Paul so that he could touch and pray over them. Many people must have been healed and delivered because scripture says and the diseases left them and the evil spirits went out of them?

As well, Elisha the prophet, was a son of God, who not only possessed a double portion of the spirit of Elijah.

2 Kings 2:9 And it came to pass, when they were gone over, that Elijah said unto Elisha, Ask what I shall do for thee, before I be taken away from thee. And Elisha said, I pray thee, let a double portion of thy spirit be upon me.

2 Kings 2:12 And Elisha saw *it,* and he cried, My father, my father, the chariot of Israel, and the horsemen thereof. And he saw him no more: and he took hold of his own clothes, and rent them in two pieces.

Elisha also carried the manifest anointing of God. The Bible records that a deceased man was about to be buried, but he was cast quickly into the grave of Elisha rather than his own grave because of sudden danger from a marauding band:

2 Kings 13:21 And it came to pass, as they were burying a man, that, behold, they spied a band *of men;* and they cast the man into the sepulchre of Elisha: and when the man was let down, and touched the bones of Elisha, he revived, and stood up on his feet.

The man was resurrected! Why? Because the manifest anointing, the lingering presence of God still lived in the very bones of Elisha, even after his death.

What amazes me is that the tangible presence of God manifests on man's flesh as well as in his bones!

So I want us to consider just how much of God's glory we can receive and manifest in our flesh as we look at this aspect in the life of God's servant, Moses. After Moses encountered God's Spirit (for 40 days and 40 nights on Mt. Sinai) he had to put a veil over his head because the radiance of God's glory shone through his face so brilliantly the people were afraid to come near him.

Exodus 34:29-35 And it came to pass, when Moses came down from mount Sinai with the two tables of testimony in Moses' hand, when he came down from the mount, that Moses wist not that the skin of his face shone while he talked with him. And when Aaron and all the children of Israel saw Moses, behold, the skin of his face shone; and they were afraid to come nigh him. And Moses called unto them; and Aaron and all the rulers of the congregation returned unto him: and Moses talked with them. And afterward all the children of Israel came nigh: and he gave them in commandment all that the LORD had spoken with him in mount Sinai. And *till* Moses had done speaking with them, he put a vail on his face. But when Moses went in before the LORD to speak with him, he took the vail off, until he came out. And he came out, and spake unto the children of Israel *that* which he was commanded. And the children of Israel saw the face of Moses, that the skin of Moses' face shone: and Moses put the vail upon his face again, until he went in to speak with him.

We need to remember that Moses was a human being (just like us) who carried the manifest glory of the Lord because he had an intimate relationship with God and he was continually in His presence. He is such a great example of someone who manifested the glory of God. And today, I believe there is a place being prepared in our hearts to receive and manifest the glory of God in a much greater capacity than ever before.

The glory of God will be seen on our flesh too if we're serious about seeking the Lord concerning this. I believe our capacity to receive and manifest the glory of God on our flesh is increasing.

As our faith for this manifestation intensifies, there is great potential for God to touch us mightily with His glory on our flesh. When God's glory shines in us and on us we'll be like lights shining in a dark world.

Isaiah 60:1-3 Arise, shine; for thy light is come, and the glory of the LORD is risen upon thee. For, behold, the darkness shall cover the earth, and gross darkness the people: but the LORD shall arise upon thee, and his glory shall be seen upon thee. And the Gentiles shall come to thy light, and kings to the brightness of thy rising.

As Christians begin manifesting the glory of God, they'll be so filled and impacted by the presence and the anointing of the Holy Spirit, that when they step into a city, literally they'll take the ground for Christ. Charles Finney, born in Connecticut in 1792 was one powerful believer who took the ground when he stepped into factories carrying the manifest anointing. All he would do is step into a factory, not saying a word, and the presence of God that he carried brought such a conviction of sin that the workers got saved. He was a dispenser of God's glory.I'm waiting for Christians, who carry the manifest presence of God, to cause demons to manifest and flee! You know, all I have to do in some crusades is start talking and the demons manifest because of the presence of God. As sons and daughters of God we can take authority over demons and bring deliverance to those who are affected by them.

The kind of anointing that I'm talking about; it will take place when we develop a God consciousness. When we see the manifestation and the revealing of the sons and daughters of God who understand who they are and what they have, they will take responsibility to defeat sin (corruption, sickness, disease, death, poverty) and to bring the glory of God with them wherever they go. Because of the glorious liberty of the children of God, believers will carry the revelation of who they are and what they have and they will be dispensers of glory.

As well, I believe God is going to bring the body of Christ together in unity, positioned to receive a corporate revelation concerning the fact that it is no longer I who live, but Christ lives in me?

Galatians 2:20 I am crucified with Christ: nevertheless I live; yet not I, but Christ liveth in me: and the life which I now live in the flesh I live by the faith of the Son of God, who loved me, and gave himself for me.

We need to be possessed by the Holy Spirit in such a way that we know it's no longer us who lives, but Christ who lives in us. And we'll be walking in this reality when Jesus actually lives through us like He wants to; through our eyes, ears, words, touch and our presence. Then the body of Christ will have a deeper revelation of what it really means to be sons and daughters of God. They will be possessed with so much of the fullness of God that they will dispense God's glory through their prayers and worship, filling the very atmosphere with the knowledge of the glory of the Lord.

Galatians 2:20 I am crucified with Christ: nevertheless I live; yet not I, but Christ liveth in me: and the life which I now live in the flesh I live by the faith of the Son of God, who loved me, and gave himself for me.

The glory will be seen like it was when the Shekinah glory filled the temple. And not only that, the glory will also be revealed in us. For I consider that the sufferings of this present time are not worthy to be compared with the glory which shall be revealed in us?

It's not just in us and to us but through us because those who He has called, He has justified and those He has justified He has glorified. And if we have this treasure in earthen vessels how much of a capacity do we have as mere men to receive and manifest the glory of God? As I said earlier, I believe we will be saturated with that glory just like Moses was.

The kingdom of heaven is at hand. And when we look at the world and the world we need to understand that the kingdoms of this world have become the kingdoms of our Lord and Christ.

Revelations 11:15 And the seventh angel sounded; and there were great voices in heaven, saying, The kingdoms of this world are become *the kingdoms* of our Lord, and of his Christ; and he shall reign for ever and ever.

The world just doesn't know it yet! Instead of looking at how defeated the world is, let's look at the potential there is for the world to become the kingdom of God. We need to understand that it's the knowledge of the glory of the Lord released through us as sons and daughters of God and the dispensers of His glory that will cause His kingdom to come on earth as it is in heaven.

When God spoke creation into existence in the beginning, He created Adam from two substances, flesh and spirit, not just a natural substance and five natural senses. So God brought two realms together, the natural realm and the heavenly realm.

When He formed man from the dust of the earth (symbolizing flesh/natural) and when He breathed into his nostrils the breath of life (symbolizing spirit/heavenly), He created man.

Genesis 2:7 And the LORD God formed man *of* the dust of the ground, and breathed into his nostrils the breath of life; and man became a living soul.

Later the Lord God fashioned a woman from the rib of the man so that he would not be alone.

Genesis 2:18 And the LORD God said, *It is* not good that the man should be alone; I will make him an help meet for him.

Genesis 2:22 And the rib, which the LORD God had taken from man, made he a woman, and brought her unto the man.

God named the man Adam and the woman Eve. Both would rule, reign, execute God's plans, and subdue and fill the earth.

Genesis 1:28 And God blessed them, and God said unto them, Be fruitful, and multiply, and replenish the earth, and subdue it: and have dominion over the fish of the sea, and over the fowl of the air, and over every living thing that moveth upon the earth.

Adam and Eve would have dominion in the earth. But their mandate had nothing to do with dominion over sin.

But much later, because of what Jesus accomplished for us through His death and resurrection, man's dominion changed so that now we have a better dominion than in the beginning. First of all, we have the opportunity to make a decision for Jesus Christ now. When we make a decision for Christ we're born again and we become new creatures; it's like we become a second creation, in the image and likeness of God. And that's when we really tap into all the inheritance and power that's available to us as sons and daughters of God. Then we have authority in the spiritual realm over sin, which includes: sickness, disease, death, poverty, Satan, demonic scorpions and serpents, every power and every evil principality.

Our kingly authority and dominion includes two realms (the natural/physical realm and the spiritual/heavenly realm) and it is much broader than the dominion Adam and Eve had in the earth in the beginning.

As born again believers we have more than the breath of God in us, the Lord Himself is in us.

Colossians 1:27 To whom God would make known what *is* the riches of the glory of this mystery among the Gentiles; which is Christ in you, the hope of glory:

Galatians 2:20 I am crucified with Christ: nevertheless I live; yet not I, but Christ liveth in me: and the life which I now live in the flesh I live by the faith of the Son of God, who loved me, and gave himself for me.

God wants us to live and have dominion, rule and reign. We are sons and daughters, ambassadors who execute the government of His kingdom over sin, sickness, disease and death. This is our role as sons and daughters of God; we are to bring the earth, with its corruption and decay, into the glorious liberty of the children of God.

Romans 8:21 Because the creature itself also shall be delivered from the bondage of corruption into the glorious liberty of the children of God.

As well, we need to take responsibility to bring the glory and the kingdom of God into the earth the same way that Jesus did 2,000 years ago. In fact, Jesus' ministry is a model of the kind of kingdom that we need to bring into the earth today. He said, He who believes in me will do the works that I do.

John 14:12 Verily, verily, I say unto you, He that believeth on me, the works that I do shall he do also; and greater *works* than these shall he do; because I go unto my Father.

It's to your advantage that I go away for if I don't go away the Holy Spirit won't come?

John 16:17 Then said *some* of his disciples among themselves, What is this that he saith unto us, A little while, and ye shall not see me: and again, a little while, and ye shall see me: and, Because I go to the Father?

What did Jesus mean? The answer is that He wants us to model the kingdom and to be the kingdom of God in the earth today.

So let's think about the greatness of God, His majesty, and go on to read another passage of scripture.

Psalms 8:1 To the chief Musician upon Gittith, A Psalm of David. O LORD our Lord, how excellent *is* thy name in all the earth! who hast set thy glory above the heavens.

Psalms 8:3-5 When I consider thy heavens, the work of thy fingers, the moon and the stars, which thou hast ordained; What is man, that thou art mindful of him? and the son of man, that thou visitest him? For thou hast made him a little lower than the angels, and hast crowned him with glory and honour.

Not only is the Lord so mindful of us that He visits us, He also cares for us when He knows our frame is but dust. When He made us, He gave us a place of honor; He made us a little lower than the angels. The word angels in some versions of the Bible is actually translated as the word God.? So I believe we have more stature than the angels and they are actually excited about what we have in Christ because they don't have what we have. They don't have the standing that we have with Him.

God put some of His honor upon us and He employs us in His providential government of the world just like David did with his sons when he made them chief rulers.

2 Samuel 8:18 And Benaiah the son of Jehoiada *was over* both the Cherethites and the Pelethites; and David's sons were chief rulers.

God made us chief rulers in the earth and He has bestowed upon us some of the glory and the honor of His kingdom.

Psalms 8:6-8 Thou madest him to have dominion over the works of thy hands; thou hast put all *things* under his feet: All sheep and oxen, yea, and the beasts of the field; The fowl of the air, and the fish of the sea, *and whatsoever* passeth through the paths of the seas.

God has employed us as ambassadors in the earth to have dominion and to bring the knowledge of the glory of the Lord as the waters cover the sea. We have dominion, not only in the natural (that's where it started in the beginning with Adam and Eve), but now because we're born again we have dominion in the spiritual realm and we become citizens of heaven.

Philippians 3:20 For our conversation is in heaven; from whence also we look for the Saviour, the Lord Jesus Christ:

Actually, we're citizens who are more involved in the heavenly realm than this Earthly realm. We're just living in our earth suit (body) and that's going to come off after a while anyway! We're a spiritual creation.

God has invited us, His spiritual creation, to partner with Him in revealing to mankind His great love and plan of salvation. Our partnership with Him began to unfold thousands of years ago when He carefully created us in His image.

Genesis 1:26 And God said, Let us make man in our image, after our likeness: and let them have dominion over the fish of the sea, and over the fowl of the air, and over the cattle, and over all the earth, and over every creeping thing that creepeth upon the earth.

We have the nature of God, the very DNA of God and the substance of God from heaven because we are created in His likeness.

From the very beginning of creation, God put the essence of Himself, His creative ability and power into the heart of every man and woman. This ability to create is the essence of who God is and what He has!

He gave these gifts to everyone, whether they believe in Him or not. The moment we were conceived in our mother's womb the Father put an ability to create inside each of us. And even though creative ability is available to every person, the power to create is especially meant for the sons and daughters of God (born-again believers). When we submit our gifts and talents to God for His glory, we're in the right position to reveal the Father's heart to mankind without fleshly motives. Man wants to be creative and is always creating inventions, music, sound, writing, kingdoms and new vision to name a few. But when creative ability is activated in the flesh without Christ, But it is true that God has put His creative ability in each one of us.

When there is real life, when believers use their gifts and talents to advance the Kingdom of God, there is great potential to influence people to make a decision for Jesus Christ. Our gifts and talents are creatively expressed both in the visible and invisible realm.

For instance, oil paintings or sculptures would be examples of expressing creativity in the visible realm. Instrumental music, or a Pastor's sermon are, creative sounds expressed in the invisible realm.

Now let's look at the creative power we have in the invisible realm concerning our speech. We hardly ever recognize that our speech is creative. When God spoke, creation happened. Let there be light and there was light. Power in His words! Words of His authority! It was Elohim, the God of creation that spoke. And Elohim, in His likeness, has created man; his likeness is in the area of the mind, will and emotions. And He created us with the ability to speak. Now here's what I want us to take to heart. Our words can bring life or death, so we need to be careful concerning what we speak because there is creative power in what we say. Whether we are saved or not, life and death is in the power of the tongue.

Creative ability or power is part of our rich inheritance from the Father. He has so much for us to tap into. As chief rulers and ambassadors, everything that He has in His kingdom is ours. But we must receive it! Remember the wayward prodigal son. The older brother got so mad because their father threw a party for his wayward little brother. The older brother complained to his father. Aw, come on! You never gave me the fattened calve, the party, the robe and the ring! And his father replied, all that I've ever had has always been yours.

Luke 15:31 And he said unto him, Son, thou art ever with me, and all that I have is thine.

But all along, the older brother didn't get it! He wasn't tapping into his inheritance the love and generosity of his father. He didn't understand who he was and what he had as a beloved son with full rights to receive great benefits from his father. His father's kingdom was always right there for the asking!

You know, so many of us are just like that older brother. We're afraid to be chief rulers and ambassadors and so we aren't enjoying all the rights and privileges that God intended for us. And so, because we still don't really understand who we are and what we have, we aren't transforming cities and nations with the glory of God. Because the Lord has employed us and given us a place of dominion, we need to realize that we have a right to be ambassadors, those who execute everything that He has given us to accomplish in His kingdom.

Concerning our position of dominion and authority, let's take a look at Psalm 82:6:

Psalms 82:6 I have said, Ye *are* **gods**; and all of you *are* children of the most High.

Notice that the word gods starts with a lower case g. So before anyone gets all freaked out, it's a small g! I feel the word gods pictures our position or rank as chief rulers and ambassadors.

This passage of scripture means that we are above all the creatures in the lower world. We have precedence over all the inhabitants of the natural earth. God made it that way. We have authority in the natural realm authority over the wind, the waves and the natural elements. We understand that. But now, through Christ, God has given us a dominion in the spirit, over sin, sickness, disease, death and poverty; this is our inheritance. He has also given us a mandate to maintain this inheritance.

Now this passage of scripture goes on to say, But you shall die like men, and fall like one of the princes.

Psalms 82:7 But ye shall die like men, and fall like one of the princes.

You know, if God really wanted to, He could take away our mandate in a moment. This verse says that we shall die like men. It's like God is saying, be careful in the midst of everything that you do. It's My name and My authority and everything that you have is only yours because I gave it to you. But you shall die like men. You shall return to the earth like dust. Yes, I visit you and I'm mindful of you. I want you to have dominion; not just dominion in the earth, but dominion in the spirit over sin, sickness, disease, death and poverty. I'm going to make you chief rulers. I want you to understand that. I'm going to give you everything; all that I ever had in the kingdom. I made you a joint-heir; our inheritance is equal.

I've given you the keys to the family car. I've given you money and the checks to the family business and I want you to manage it. If you're not being a good manager and steward of what I've given you, if you're not representing the kingdom in a godly, righteous way, I can come back and say, give me the car. Give me the keys. Give me the checks. So we need to be careful to respect the Lord God, the one who made us who we are and the one who gave us what we have.

Yes, God wants us to respect Him and our mandate; to be dispensers of glory and those who bring creation itself into glorious liberty of the children of God.

Romans 8:19-29 For the earnest expectation of the creature waiteth for the manifestation of the sons of God. For the creature was made subject to vanity, not willingly, but by reason of him who hath subjected *the same* in hope, Because the creature itself also shall be delivered from the bondage of corruption into the glorious liberty of the children of God. For we know that the whole creation groaneth and travaileth in pain together until now. And not only *they,* but ourselves also, which have the firstfruits of the Spirit, even we ourselves groan within ourselves, waiting for the adoption, *to wit,* the redemption of our body. For we are saved by hope: but hope that is seen is not hope: for what a man seeth, why doth he yet hope for? But if we hope for that we see not, *then* do we with patience wait for *it.* Likewise the Spirit also helpeth our infirmities: for we know not what we should pray for as we ought: but the Spirit itself maketh intercession for us with groanings which cannot be uttered. And he that searcheth the hearts knoweth what *is* the mind of the Spirit, because he maketh intercession for the saints according to *the will of* God. And we know that all things work together for good to them that love God, to them who are the called according to *his* purpose. For whom he did foreknow, he also did predestinate *to be* conformed to the image of his Son, that he might be the firstborn among many brethren.

He wants us to know that we are chosen to do the works of Jesus and even greater works than He did. I want to discuss a segment from the life of John G. Lake because he was a dispenser of God's glory and one who knew who he was and what He had. He understood the greater works that Jesus spoke of.

In the early 1900's John G. Lake began a powerful healing ministry. When he ministered in Spokane there were so many people healed that the authorities declared Spokane to be the healthiest city in America! God did amazing feats through this man. Over 100,000 documented healings and miracles happened in just five years of his ministry in that city. Healing parades were organized. Trucks would be loaded up with people who were healed of different infirmities.

One truck would carry those healed of cancer; another truck would carry those healed of deafness, and another truck with those who had been blind and so on. The hospitals were almost put out of business!

Many of us not only respect John G. Lake's ministry, we respect John G. Lake, the apostle. In South Africa, as a result of his ministry in that region, over 600 churches were planted in five years. The healing anointing he carried literally touched people from all over the world. Even his ministry newsletters carried the manifest presence of God. Before his newsletters went out in the mail, his staff would bring them to him. Then, with great conviction, John G. Lake would say,

I want to pray and I only want men who are in contact with the Living God to pray with me, nobody else. Together we're going to lay our bodies on these newsletters like Elisha the prophet laid on that dead child's body?

As everyone prayed like he commanded, the power of God literally permeated the very paper until the very fabric of that paper was saturated with the power and presence of the manifest anointing. The lightening of God would flash through the souls of those who prayed and the power of God would be released on those newsletters. Then Lake's ministry would send them out all over the world. When some people touched their newsletter, they would fall under the power, speak in tongues and get healed! So, when people asked Lake what the secret was to his anointing he said, It's God consciousness. I believe it's possible to know and practice, like John G. Lake did, the secret to manifesting the anointing through God consciousness.

As well, we need to understand the depth of what Jesus meant when He prayed Holy Father, keep them in Your name, the name which You have given Me, that they may be one even as We are.

John 17:11 And now I am no more in the world, but these are in the world, and I come to thee. Holy Father, keep through thine own name those whom thou hast given me, that they may be one, as we *are.*

I believe we can experience oneness with God, just like John G. Lake did. Jesus prayed that we would be one. When we really comprehend Jesus' high priestly prayer, then we'll feel His heart beat. We'll understand what He's doing and what it takes to partner with Him.

John G. Lake believed that Christians should minister in the same type of power that Jesus did while He lived on earth. The church is supposed to be a living, visible expression of what Jesus looked like 2,000 years ago! The church is the body of Christ and it needs to emerge in the earth today as a company of people who are manifesting the anointing. God wants us to realize that the anointing isn't just for a few individuals, but rather, it's available for the body of Christ!

The church is His body! So it's like God is saying, I want the body, the church, not just the evangelist, pastor, prophet, teacher, Bill

Vincent manifesting the anointing. It's the corporate anointing. It's the five fold training and equipping of the saints to do the work of the ministry until we all come into the unity of the faith. So what's God's plan? It's that we all come into the unity of the faith, into the fullness, into the maturity, into the stature of Christ.

Ephesians 1:17-23 That the God of our Lord Jesus Christ, the Father of glory, may give unto you the spirit of wisdom and revelation in the knowledge of him: The eyes of your understanding being enlightened; that ye may know what is the hope of his calling, and what the riches of the glory of his inheritance in the saints, And what *is* the exceeding greatness of his power to us-ward who believe, according to the working of his mighty power, Which he wrought in Christ, when he raised him from the dead, and set *him* at his own right hand in the heavenly *places,* Far above all principality, and power, and might, and dominion, and every name that is named, not only in this world, but also in that which is to come: And hath put all *things* under his feet, and gave him *to be* the head over all *things* to the church, Which is his body, the fulness of him that filleth all in all.

You know, the nations of old would look with dread at the children of Israel and say, Oh my goodness! Moses is coming! He's leading a vast company of people!? The terror that came upon the nations was because they were a race of people emerging as a nation accompanied by the presence of God.

Deuteronomy 26:8 And the LORD brought us forth out of Egypt with a mighty hand, and with an outstretched arm, and with great terribleness, and with signs, and with wonders:

And wisely, Moses didn't want to go anywhere without God's presence, because it made the children of Israel distinct from all other people.

Exodus 33:15, 16 And he said unto him, If thy presence go not *with me,* carry us not up hence. For wherein shall it be known here that I and thy people have found grace in thy sight? *is it* not in that thou goest with us? so shall we be separated, I and thy people, from all the people that *are* upon the face of the earth.

Moses knew that one major distinguishing mark (that made them different from any other nation and religion) was the fact that God was with them. When the nations looked at the children of Israel they saw, not just individuals, but a whole company of people led by their God. They saw God!

The secular world sees the body of Christ manifesting the anointing, they'll see God too! But if we're not taking our place or taking our authority (as chief rulers and ambassadors) to advance God's kingdom, then the world will just see the church as an ineffective institution and lump us in with all the other religions. The world needs to see our distinguishing marks!

One distinguishing mark is that the presence of God leads us and goes with us. Another mark is that the body of Christ is a living expression of what Jesus was like 2,000 years ago when he cast out devils, preached the gospel, healed the sick, raised the dead and moved in kingdom power. The church is meant to know the love of Christ which passes knowledge; that you may be filled with all the fullness of God.

Ephesians 3:19 And to know the love of Christ, which passeth knowledge, that ye might be filled with all the fulness of God.

So the church is supposed to be all the fullness of everything that Jesus is. But we're not. Yet that's God's will. All the fullness of God! Can you imagine what that looks like?

Why would Paul the apostle pray that we would be filled up with all the fullness of God? He's talking to Christians already filled with the Spirit and already moving in the anointing. But what if the Spirit is given in measure? Paul spoke about the measure of our full stature: until we all come to the unity of the faith and of the knowledge of the Son of God, to a perfect man, to the measure of the stature of the fullness of Christ.

Ephesians 4:13 Till we all come in the unity of the faith, and of the knowledge of the Son of God, unto a perfect man, unto the measure of the stature of the fulness of Christ:

Jesus had the Spirit without measure. So that means the anointing comes to us in measure.

John 3:34 For he whom God hath sent speaketh the words of God: for God giveth not the Spirit by measure *unto him.*

Yes, we have the Spirit with measure, but there is more of the Spirit available to us.

That's why Paul was praying that we would be filled with the fullness of God because we're still not walking in the fullness of everything that we can receive and manifest on the earth now; there's great potential for much more. We still need the revelation of what it means to be filled with the fullness of God and to understand who we are and what we have.

Jesus Himself had the fullness of the Godhead in the flesh. In Jesus dwelt all the fullness of the Godhead.

Colossians 1:19 For it pleased *the Father* that in him should all fulness dwell;

John 1:16 And of his fulness have all we received, and grace for grace.

God wants us to enter into more of the fullness of everything that He has for us. Sometimes our limited mindset and understanding concerning how deep we can go with God hinders us from enjoying the great inheritance that is ours in Christ Jesus. Believers will often set limits concerning the fullness of who God is.

Then they never really tap into their inheritance and the power that God wants us as his sons and daughters to receive and manifest.

In fact, the kingdom of God is within us and I want to declare that the kingdom of heaven is at hand. Because Paul the apostle prayed that we would be filled with all the fullness of God, it's obvious that we aren't yet filled with all the fullness. That means there is always more available for us. I'm never satisfied with where I've been or what I've had in the past. I want more and I'm pressing in for more because I know I have a great capacity inside of me that longs for the fullness of God. I believe that our capacity for more of the fullness can be stretched far and wide until we're walking in the kind of anointing that Jesus walked in 2,000 years ago. The anointing that Peter and Paul had is also for us! We can have the same kind of anointing that Moses walked in; our faces can shine with God's glory so when the world rubs shoulders with us they come close to the presence of God because He is with us.

2 Corinthians 3:7, 8 But if the ministration of death, written *and* engraven in stones, was glorious, so that the children of Israel could not stedfastly behold the face of Moses for the glory of his countenance; which *glory* was to be done away: How shall not the ministration of the spirit be rather glorious?

When the body of Christ manifests the anointing so strongly that bar patrons can't get their beers off the bar table to their mouth, then the world will see Jesus in us, the hope of glory! When we understand what it takes to be sons and daughters of God in the fullness of the Spirit of God, like Finney, we'll walk into a factory and without saying one word the whole factory will be saved. Let's press in to receive a whole lot more of the fullness of the Spirit of God in our lives!

God wants us to tap into all of the fullness of what He has for us as His sons and daughters.

We need a holy hunger that drives us to go the distance with God because the whole earth, creation itself, is waiting for the manifestation and the revealing of the sons and daughters of God. So this week we're going to dig into some practical keys to release the anointing so that we can express the heart of Jesus to mankind.

There's a groaning and a cry from creation itself for deliverance and power: I want to be set free! I want to throw off the curse of the law and disease and death! Oh where are the sons and daughters of God? Where are the people who are dispensers of the glory who can do something about death because they carry resurrection power? Where are the people who will bring creation itself into the glorious liberty of the children of God? The Lord wants to answer this cry by a rising up of radical Christians who will take responsibility to advance His kingdom.

This company of believers, the body of Christ, will come into their position as, chief rulers and ambassadors of the kingdom of heaven here on earth. It's God's desire that the body of Christ would arise with a passion to be an expression to the world of what Jesus was like 2,000 years ago. So often we have a rapture departure mentality! We need to break that mentality; otherwise we're not going to walk in the fullness of which we are now and what we have. It's like we're constantly saying, I can't wait until God gets us out of this mess; maybe just ten more years, maybe just twenty more years. Or, I believe Jesus is going to come in my lifetime. Well that's great, but what are we doing now to advance the kingdom of God?

Yes, Jesus is coming. I want Jesus to come too. But I'm not even concerned about that because I'm too busy sweating in the harvest field to look up and see if He's coming. I'm trying to get as many as I can into the kingdom of God before He gets here. And I'm not in a hurry for Jesus to get here because I know where I am going.

I'm not in any hurry to get out of my body and into heaven; I'm living in heaven now as much as I want to. The kingdom of heaven is at hand. The kingdom of heaven is within us.

And as I said before, we're a spiritual creation. We have spiritual eyes called the eyes of our understanding. We touch, taste, smell, hear, and see in the natural and in the spiritual. We are citizens of heaven possessing everything that heaven has to offer. We have the opportunity before us to be full with all the fullness of God because we are sons and daughters of God. We're joint heirs with an inheritance.

Everything in the natural realm and everything in the spiritual realm is under our feet because Elohim has made us just a little lower than Himself.

Psalms 8:5 For thou hast made him a little lower than the angels, and hast crowned him with glory and honour.

Because we have dominion in the spirit over sin, sickness, disease, death and poverty there is an invitation to come boldly before God's throne and to partner with Him by taking our position of authority. So let's examine some of the keys that will release the anointing in our lives. We want to be dispensers of God's glory who take responsibility for the ministry that God has for us.

Consciousness means: the state of being conscious; awareness or the totality of one's thoughts and feelings (Webster's Dictionary). We'll have a deep God consciousness and awareness of God's will and what He's doing in the present moment when we are: walking in holiness, saturated by the Holy Spirit, abiding in the vine close to the Father's heart, keenly aware of the prompting and quickening of the Holy Spirit.

It's God's desire that the body of Christ possess the same kind of anointing that John G. Lake had. So I have a question. Just how badly do we want it?

Through His Spirit which dwells in us, the anointing is released. It doesn't get anymore practical than this: But if the Spirit of Him who raised Jesus from the dead dwells in you, He who raised Christ from the dead will also give life to your mortal bodies through His Spirit who dwells in you? The Holy Spirit will bring life and healing power not only to our mortal bodies through the Spirit who dwells in us, He will bring His life and healing power to those we pray for. When the power of God comes upon us, it's released out of the spirit realm into our soul realm. Then it manifests into our bodies and our sickness falls off.

If we meditate on the scripture passage just mentioned, the living word of God will become a reality that permeates our whole being.

Here's what I say when I'm lying on my bed

meditating on a verse like this: The same Spirit, the very same Spirit that anointed Jesus to heal all those oppressed of the Devil, that same Spirit that anointed and empowered the ministry of Jesus, that raised Jesus from the dead, lives in me! In me right now is the very same Spirit that raised His dead body 2,000 years ago! The very same Spirit that was involved in the creation of the universe itself; the same Spirit!?

So when I begin to meditate on: Christ in me; the sons and daughters of God; God consciousness; being possessed by God; the authority and power that's in me by God's Spirit; all of a sudden the anointing begins to well up in me like a spring called living water. Then it becomes rivers of living water flowing through my body and soul. So I get healed and so does everyone else around me! (You know what? We can even practice this on an airplane. Just sit there, get quiet and start releasing Christ in you until the guy next to you starts to feel Him. We can have a lot of fun partnering with the Holy Spirit this way.)

The fact is that God made us to partner with Him. When we get a solid revelation about this I believe we will see a lot more of the power of

God. So often when Christians start talking about the power of God they say, it's Jesus. Look to Jesus!? Everything we have is because He gave it to us and He made us joint heirs. But God made us to partner with Him and He doesn't want us to be timid. We are co-laborers with Him and we don't have to apologize for this! We can be bold!

When I'm in a meeting I'll ask God, Who do you want to heal right now? And then I can actually see who will get healed at that moment and I tell that person to stand up. I'll say to them, whatever is wrong with your body will be healed right now! And healing will happen because I'll actually see the Spirit of the Lord hovering over them and I'll recognize there is an anointing for healing and then I'll boldly declare it.

The apostles Peter and John co-labored with God boldly. Once they came upon a lame man who wanted alms from them. But Peter and John had something much better to give him. Both apostles said to the man, Look at us!? US! So the lame man gave them his attention because he expected to receive their alms. But instead of giving him mere money, Peter' eyes pierced the man's soul as he said, Silver and gold I do not have. But what I do have I give you in the name of Jesus Christ of Nazareth. Rise up and walk? Now watch this! Peter didn't have silver and gold, but he declared boldly what I do have I give you. His boldness came forth without hesitation because he knew who he was and what God said he had and so he commanded the man in Jesus Name to walk! And with a leap the man stood upright and began walking. Healed!

Now even though Peter knew he was God's partner, his boldness could have looked like pride to an onlooker. Hey wait a minute Peter. I thought Jesus was the healer. Why are you telling the man to look at you? We better get our eyes on Jesus. Yes, we're supposed to fix our eyes on Jesus. And I believe Peter and John were doing just that in their hearts as they boldly commanded the lame man to look at them. There comes a time when we understand who we are and what we have and it makes us bold in Jesus.

There's an anointing that takes us beyond just asking for something in prayer. It's called the authoritative command. Here's how the authoritative command works in the area of healing. We tell the body what to do! Listen to what Jesus commanded His disciples: Heal the sick.

Matthew 10:8 Heal the sick, cleanse the lepers, raise the dead, cast out devils: freely ye have received, freely give.

Jesus didn't say, Pray for the sick. He said, Heal the sick. In other words, we have the authority to command the body what to do.

The authoritative command of healing isn't, Lord, I pray for this cancer to be healed. Or, Jesus, I pray for this guy to be set free and that you take off all the chains. Or, Oh Jesus, I pray that you take the devil out of this guy's body. No! It's the authoritative command of healing. We can command diseases to leave: Cancer, in the name of Jesus I say to leave this body!'

As well, it's not about wondering if it's God's will to heal someone, or even asking if He wants to use us as an instrument to bring healing. We don't pray about it, rather we prophecy the word with creative power. (God put creative power within us the moment we were created. So now we begin to take our authority and say take up your bed and walk!

Tumor in this body, I command you in Jesus name to wither and die right now! Viruses in this body, be cursed, wither and die! Burn now, virus!

God will hear the cry of a person who doesn't know how to pray and they just cry Help! He comes in mercy and love. I believe that! God's grace can make up for any weakness. But I still believe there is still a place for the Spirit of the Lord God is upon me because He has anointed me, to do what to proclaim liberty to the captives.

To say to those who sit in darkness, Come forth!? I stopped praying for people to get saved. I just command them! As I step into what God reveals to me and issue authoritative commands because I know who I am and what I have, boldness rises within me. Also, because I know I'm a son of God and the Father loves me just as much as He loves Jesus, I'm not afraid of the Devil. Jesus prayed, and that the world may know that You have sent Me, and have loved them as You have loved Me? Do we understand what He said? He's the firstborn, our brother! And now we're joint heirs and co-laborers. So we take our authority. We're made for dominion; we're made to conquer and overcome. We're chief rulers who possess authority over sin, sickness, disease, death and poverty.

We have authority over the spiritual atmosphere.

Before I minister in a service I'll begin to take authority over the spiritual climate because I have an understanding concerning the connection between demons and sickness. I'll bind and take authority over demons that cause different sicknesses.

Ephesians 6:12 For we wrestle not against flesh and blood, but against principalities, against powers, against the rulers of the darkness of this world, against spiritual wickedness in high *places.*

Then I'll command those devils to let go of the people and I'll release a corporate anointing. People will get healed in their seats the moment we bind and loose in heaven.

An intimate relationship with the Holy Spirit is the key to receiving words of knowledge. I began to flow in this gift (Word of Knowledge) after spending lots of time developing a relationship with the Holy Spirit.

It was during this intense season that I began to develop my spiritual senses. And even to this day I will wait on the Lord. I'll take maybe 10 minutes, or it could be an hour and sometimes three hours at a time to lie before Him.

The word of knowledge is simply when we get synchronized with the blue print of heaven; what's happening in heaven at that precise moment. Jesus describes this as the spirit of counsel and might.

Isaiah 11:2 And the spirit of the LORD shall rest upon him, the spirit of wisdom and understanding, the spirit of counsel and might, the spirit of knowledge and of the fear of the LORD;

Might is strength and power and the spirit of counsel is wisdom and revelation. I only want to do things that I see my Father doing. That brings the Spirit of power.

John 5:19 Then answered Jesus and said unto them, Verily, verily, I say unto you, The Son can do nothing of himself, but what he seeth the Father do: for what things soever he doeth, these also doeth the Son likewise.

So before I come into a service, I'll take between one and three hours to be quiet before the Lord, seeking Him concerning the blueprint of heaven for the service. He will always speak.

As I seek the Lord I'll begin to just know things and I'll get impressions that I feel in my body. I'll see visions, pictures, or open visions and sometimes I'll get inner or outer visions and trances where I'll fall into a dream like state, but I'm awake. I'll just know things in his presence. His presence brings an impartation of the spirit of wisdom and revelation; the spirit of knowledge and understanding..

Here are two keys that will help us to release words of knowledge. The first key concerns a lifestyle of sowing into the kingdom of God. God is a rewarder of those who diligently seek Him; those who sow into His kingdom. The second key is to confidently ask God for details. You see, after the Lord gives me an impression about someone, I will ask for more information.

Are they male or female? And then I'll keep pressing in by asking God where they will be sitting in the service and what their name is. I'll continue asking for details and making myself available to the Lord as I wait in faith for His revelation.

Then as He responds and begins to show me things, I initiate back in the faith realm. So it goes from faith realm to sovereign realm to faith realm. As God begins to show me things, I begin to pull for more details. Sometimes He'll give me the whole thing and other times He'll give me a piece. And because I am not satisfied with a piece, I'll ask more questions: What is their middle name? What is their last name? Who are they connected to? And God may give me the word of knowledge. Now when I come into a meeting and I declare that word as I saw it heaven, the power of God is released on the earth. As the word of knowledge goes forth it brings great encouragement, healing and deliverance. But it's only because I synchronized heaven and earth.

Look for what the Father is doing. After I release a corporate anointing for healing, I'll ask, who's feeling something in their body right now: fire, heat, electricity. Or, who knows their pain is gone and you're able to do something you couldn't do before? I want you to respond to what's happening right now. And then even as they begin to respond, I pray for God to bless and continue what the Father is doing.

Two or three people will often report the same kind of healing. An example would be that several are healed of an ear condition and so I'll know this is a common thread. I've learned to look for common threads when I want to release the anointing. So if there is a common grouping of certain kinds of miracles taking place by the sovereign hand of God, then I will pray for everybody with that condition in that moment. This is the way that I will know what the Father is doing.

Sometimes when I am in a service like this, when I want to manifest and release the anointing in worship or when I take the microphone, I'll say, let's wait on the Lord for a moment. I'll look around the room, watching for the visible touch of the Lord on somebody. Sometimes I'll see a pocket of three people in one area and to say, there's a pocket of three people over here; the anointing is on this side of the room. And then I'll come over and capitalize on what's happening. And then I'll take that little pocket and whoosh it down the row. We need to learn how to be sensitive to feel and read the room to know what's going on and we need to look around to see and discern what the Father is doing.

Learn to recognize and discern a different anointing on people's lives. Because I've have developed a sensitivity to the Spirit of God I can look over a crowd and recognize a different anointing. I've come to know and feel a anointing.

(It's a knowing and isn't like seeing someone with your physical eyes.) I might discern a prophetic anointing or a healing anointing on someone. Or I might see an anointing for the joy of the Lord and refreshing. Often I'll call out someone's destiny. I might see music over somebody or have a strong impression they are apostolic or prophetic. The ability to recognize a different anointing is a great gift from the Lord because people get so encouraged to press on in their walk with the Lord and to continue to step out in their anointing.

People usually don't realize that when they have the gift of faith it can actually be seen on them! When Paul the apostle was preaching in Lystra, he saw a lame man who had faith to be healed.

Acts 14:9 The same heard Paul speak: who stedfastly beholding him, and perceiving that he had faith to be healed,

I thought about that. Was the man doing something in the natural that caused Paul to see that he had faith? So I asked the Lord how Paul knew about the lame man's faith. And the Lord revealed that Paul saw the substance; faith is the substance. He saw the spirit of faith.

Here's how I see someone's faith. When I want to release God's power in a meeting I'll actually look over the room to see if there is anyone who has faith. I can actually look at people and see what some would call an aura or energy. (That's what the world will call it.) When I see a substance like electricity hovering over someone, I'll say, the spirit of faith is on you. Come on up here. And they'll get healed. At times I'll actually look for that substance in people's eyes.

Now we all have faith, but we aren't all in the gift of faith. Here's the difference. We have faith, but that's the faith we all have because God dealt to each one a measure of faith? But it's not the supernatural energy of faith the gift of faith that's an actual infusion of energy that comes upon someone to believe God. When this hits someone, I can see it happening in the room.

I'll know if someone has the gift of faith functioning, or if they have normal faith. We don't grow the gift of faith because it's given to us as a perfect complete gift. On the other hand, the faith that God has dealt to each one of us in measure, can grow.

When believers manifest the anointing, they will release the anointing! God wants us to know who we are and what we have as sons and daughters who are called to be chief rulers and ambassadors in the earth. As we walk in the fullness of what the Lord intended for us, we'll be a company of people who manifest the anointing to the extent that cities and nations are impacted by the gospel.

ABOUT THE AUTHOR

Bill Vincent is no stranger to understanding the power of God. Not only has he spent over twenty years as a Minister with a strong prophetic anointing, he is now also an Apostle and Author with Revival Waves of Glory Ministries in Litchfield, IL. Along with his wife, Tabitha, he, leads a team providing apostolic oversight in all aspects of ministry, including service, personal ministry and Godly character.

Bill offers a wide range of writings and teachings from deliverance, to experiencing presence of God and developing Apostolic cutting edge Church structure. Drawing on the power of the Holy Spirit through years of experience in Revival, Spiritual Sensitivity, and deliverance ministry, Bill now focuses mainly on pursuing the Presence of God and breaking the power of the devil off of people's lives.

His books 48 and counting has since helped many people to overcome the spirits and curses of Satan. For more information or to keep up with Bill's latest releases, please visit www.revivalwavesofgloryministries.com. To contact Bill, feel free to follow him on twitter @revivalwaves.

RECOMMENDED PRODUCTS

By Bill Vincent

Overcoming Obstacles
Glory: Pursuing God's Presence
Defeating the Demonic Realm
Increasing Your Prophetic Gift
Increasing Your Anointing
Keys to Receiving Your Miracle
The Supernatural Realm
Waves of Revival
Increase of Revelation and Restoration
The Resurrection Power of God
Discerning Your Call of God
Apostolic Breakthrough
Glory: Increasing God's Presence
Love is Waiting – Don't Let Love Pass You By
The Healing Power of God
Glory: Expanding God's Presence
Receiving Personal Prophecy
Signs and Wonders
Signs and Wonders Revelations
Children Stories
The Rapture
The Secret Place of God's Power
Building a Prototype Church
Breakthrough of Spiritual Strongholds
Glory: Revival Presence of God

Increasing Your Anointing

Overcoming the Power of Lust
Glory: Kingdom Presence of God
Transitioning Into a Prototype Church
The Stronghold of Jezebel
Healing After Divorce
A Closer Relationship With God
Cover Up and Save Yourself
Desperate for God's Presence
The War for Spiritual Battles
Spiritual Leadership
Global Warning
There Are Millions of Churches
Destroying the Jezebel Spirit
Awakening of Miracles
Deception and Consequences Revealed
Are You a Follower of Christ
Don't Let the Enemy Steal from You!
A Godly Shaking
The Unsearchable Riches of Christ
Heaven's Court System
Satan's Open Doors
Armed for Battle
The Wrestler
Spiritual Warfare: Complete Collection
Growing In the Prophetic
The Prototype Church: Complete Edition
Faith
The Rapture

To Order:

Email:

rwgcontact@yahoo.com

Web Site:

www.revivalwavesofgloryministries.com

Mail Order:

Revival Waves of Glory
PO Box 596
Litchfield, IL 62056

Shipping $5.00

If you mail an order and pay by check, make check out to Revival Waves of Glory.

Most books are in multiple formats such as Hardcover, Soft-Cover, Ebook (such as Kindle & Nook), and Audio Books.

SD - #0019 - 070726 - C0 - 216/138/7 - PB - 9780692648889 - Gloss Lamination